A Special Gift

Presented to:

....

from:

....

date:

....

Sayings, Scriptures, and Stories from
the Bible Revealing God's Love

hugs
from
Heaven

Embraced

by the

Savior

HOWARD
PUBLISHING CO.

Caron Loveless

Our purpose at Howard Publishing is to:

- *Increase faith* in the hearts of growing Christians
- *Inspire holiness* in the lives of believers
- *Instill hope* in the hearts of struggling people everywhere

Because He's coming again!

Hugs from Heaven, Embraced by the Savior
© 1998 by Caron Loveless
All rights reserved. Printed in the United States of America

Published by Howard Publishing Co., Inc.,
3117 North 7th Street, West Monroe, LA 71291-2227

00 01 02 03 04 05 06 07   10 9 8 7 6

Paraphrased Scriptures by LeAnn Weiss, owner of Encouragement Company, 3006 Brandywine Dr., Orlando, FL 32806

Interior Design by Stephanie Denney
Edited by Janet Reed

Library of Congress Cataloging-in-Publication Data
Loveless, Caron, 1955-
    Hugs from heaven, embraced by the Savior : sayings, scriptures,
and stories from the Bible revealing God's love / Caron Loveless ;
personalized scriptures by LeAnn Weiss.
      p. cm.
    ISBN 1-878990-91-8
    1. God—Love. 2. Bible stories, English—N.T. Gospels.
I. Weiss, LeAnn. II. Title.
BT140.L685 1998
242—dc21   98-38160
                                              CIP

Contents

Introduction

The *Hugs from Heaven Series* is written with one purpose in mind: to make God's love more real and refreshing to your heart and spirit than ever before. The book is divided into topical sections consisting of a paraphrased scripture, an inspirational message, a poignant saying, and a fictional story based on a particular passage of scripture. Even though the narrative is fictional, and the writer takes a creative course with the story, the biblical truths are uncompromised. Favorite Bible stories take on new meaning as you are transported to the scene to explore the thoughts and feelings of the men and women who were touched by heaven's embrace in a special way. May the message in this book, and all of the *Hugs from Heaven* books, bring honor to our God and praise to the Savior, Jesus Christ.

one

His
Restoring
Embrace

Don't get discouraged. I'm close to the brokenhearted, and I specialize in rescuing you when you're crushed in spirit. Your weakness is the perfect opportunity for my power to shine. Meanwhile, I give you my all-sufficient grace.

Your God of Deliverance

—from Psalm 34:18; 2 Corinthians 12:9

Embraced by the Savior

"*Dear Lord, give me the grace to remember that you are ready to embrace me, if I am willing to take one step toward you.*"

—*John Cowan*

Somewhere along the way we've latched on to the idea that broken is bad. It probably started in our childhood when we got the glare for breaking Aunt Wilma's Waterford crystal or when the angry neighbor came over to ask if we knew about his shattered living room window. Maybe it was reinforced when we heard a parent yell, "Do you have any idea how much that toy costs!" However it happened, we learned our lesson; broken things really bother and embarrass us. We wear hats on bad hair days, hide broken fingernails, dump sour marriages, and avoid hospital visits. It's funny when you think about it. We're born into a cracked up, broken-down world.

4

You'd think we'd feel more at home in it. Jesus did. Of all people, you'd think he'd have a problem with anything less than perfection. But Jesus seemed attracted to it! In fact, he made it pretty clear he hadn't come to visit the neatly put together types. The sickly, unseemly ones drew his attention. Christ let everyone know what he thought of blind eyes and deaf ears and broken hearts: They didn't repel him; they compelled him. And two thousand years hasn't changed his mind about us. He'd still rather dine with the destitute, call on the crippled, and welcome the wayward. It's hard to comprehend sometimes, isn't it?

We see the sorry, shattered pieces of our lives and conclude we're finished. But the Savior sees those same pieces, lays them flat in the palm of his hand, solders them together with his love, and then stands back to let the light of his glory stream through a brand-new stained-glass window. Don't be ashamed of your brokenness. It's fresh material for a masterpiece. Through your weakness God's strength is most brilliantly seen.

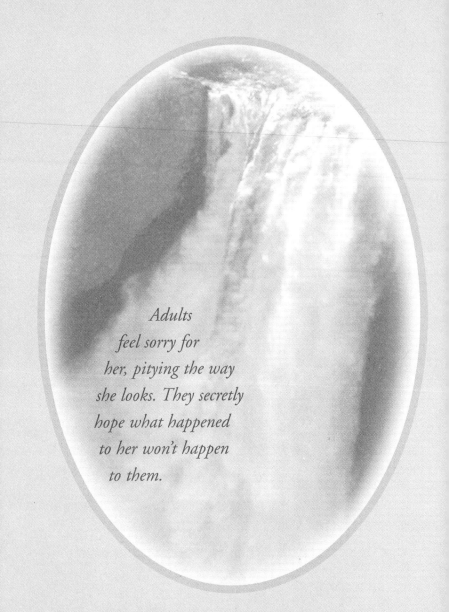

Adults
feel sorry for
her, pitying the way
she looks. They secretly
hope what happened
to her won't happen
to them.

Yes, I Mean You

She frightens little children. They run and hide or bury their faces in their mothers' skirts when they see her coming. Adults feel sorry for her, pitying the way she looks. As she goes on her way, they secretly hope what happened to her won't happen to them.

The woman didn't always look this way. In her teens, she laughed and lived like other young girls. She dreamed of marriage one day. She even collected linens and dishes from her grandmother and stored them away, waiting for the right man to come along. But he didn't get there in time. Instead of a suitor, a serious, disfiguring disease came knocking on her door. Within months it took up permanent residence in her body.

Though the doctors pronounced her incurable, she was young and hopeful. She searched for a treatment to reverse the painful, grotesque curvature of her back. But her efforts were futile.

The discomfort and embarrassment have been with her for eighteen years.

"Why don't you come live with us?" her sister says at least once a month. "You can hardly reach into the cabinets. How long can you manage alone like this?"

"I do all right," the woman replies. "My garden keeps me busy. You'd be surprised how productive you can be when you don't have to stop and straighten your back every five minutes. Besides, you know the saying: The shepherd carries the crippled sheep on his shoulders. He looks after me."

Every week, without fail, the woman makes the long trek to worship. She shuffles her feet on the familiar route, hunched over, clacking her cane on the cobblestones. Why is she so faithful? She finds rest in the room and comfort in the words. The repetitive rhythms and ancient sounds soothe her soul. The Scriptures make her feel whole.

But today something peculiar is happening. The room is full, flowing over into the street. Buzzing through the crowd is news that a gifted teacher has come to read from the law and reason from the prophets. He must be good, the woman thinks. Even a few well-known Gentiles have gathered to listen.

Her curiosity rises a bit but falls quickly as she realizes her usual seat might be taken.

"Make way here," she says, boldly swinging her stick. "Let an old woman through." She pokes and jabs with her cane until a young man with a baby in his arms grudgingly

9

steps aside. One by one the group parts as if Moses himself had commanded it.

In her healthy days, the woman was average height. Now with her back bent over, she's almost the size of a child. In the crammed space she looks like David in a land of Goliaths. When she finally reaches her spot, it's taken. She'll have to resort to leaning against a corner in the back of the room. She won't be able to see the teacher, but hearing him, she decides, is better than nothing.

Looking between the heads of eager townsmen and past presiding elders, Jesus locks his gaze on the bent woman. He traces each halting step. He notes each wincing breath. And with the ultimate X-ray look, he determines which evil spirit is assigned to her body.

His disciples know something's up. They've seen this look in his eyes before. He's intent, focused, and apparently troubled. They can tell he's seen something in the back of the room. A demon, maybe? They look and see a scrambling assortment of bodies. But Jesus sees only one.

Its pain and disorder wound his heart, and mercy seeps from the Savior.

He takes a step forward. The disciples hush the crowd.

"Woman, come here," Jesus says gently. Every woman within earshot looks his way until all but one discovers he's calling someone else.

"I think he's talking to you," a young girl says, pulling on the woman's sleeve.

"Me?" the woman answers. "What would he want with me?"

Jesus stands alone at the front of the room, smiling. It's the kind of smile people use when they know a secret or they're holding back a surprise. He stretches his arm out to the woman with his palm turned up. Seeing her quizzical look he says, "Yes, I mean you. Come here."

Heads turn and eyes fix on the deformed woman as she squeezes through the crowd once again. Maybe he'll pray for her, some think. Maybe he'll give a special blessing for enduring so well for so long.

"This is a break from our usual order. What does he think he's doing?" one of the elders whispers.

The woman stands before Jesus, bent and baffled but obedient. She's not afraid. There's something familiar in the teacher's voice, something settling in his eyes. The room becomes noiseless except for the whining of a child.

Then Jesus speaks—not a long lecture, not a fiery incantation. He speaks eight everyday words that, from the mouth of the Almighty, incite enough power to shake her world straight. With boldness he says, "Woman, you are free from your infirmity." And the Captain of the Lord's Host reaches out to touch her crooked frame and snap it to attention.

A gasp goes up from the crowd as a torch blows down her spine. The disciples blink, the elders gulp, a young girl screams, and the woman jumps. In one split second her deformity is dismantled, demolished, disposed of. In the time it takes to catch your breath, the woman who had hung her head down for eighteen years is now free to lift it boldly toward heaven.

Just as her disease had come, so came her healing. She never expected it. She didn't even ask for it. But out of compassion, Christ offered and delivered it to her in person.

And he's still in the delivery business . . . worldwide.

A broken body and a shattered soul may be the last things we want to be known for. But they're the first things that get God's attention. When we can't stand up, we stand out. The Savior sees every mangled wreck we've made in our lives. He offers to use his "Jaws of Life" to cut away the debris and lead us to a safe, secure place.

Rest assured, you've caught his eye. Be at peace. You've captured his heart. Even if you're sitting in the back of the room, he sees you. And if you shush the racket inside you and ignore the enemy's distractions, right now, in this moment, you can hear him say, "Come here. Come to me. Yes, I mean you."

Scriptural Account

On Sabbath Jesus was teaching in one of the synagogues, and a woman was there who had been crippled by a spirit for eighteen years. She was bent over and could not straighten up at all. When Jesus saw her, he called her forward and said to her, "Woman, you are set free from your infirmity." Then he put his hands on her, and immediately she straightened up and praised God.

—*Luke 13:10–13*

two

His Refreshing Embrace

"Don't dwell on your past. I'm in the business of making things new. My compassions and mercies never fail. They are new every morning. Watch me make roadways in your wilderness. My gushing rivers are coming to bring refreshment to your parched and empty life. It may seem like just a trickle at first, but soon it will spring up and bubble over. You've been chosen to drink of my living water.

Your God of Abundant Life
—from Isaiah 43:18–20; Lamentations 3:22–23

Embraced by the Savior

"One quickly gains a sense from the Bible that wherever the Holy Spirit is found in the lives of people, strange and wonderful things are likely to happen at any moment."

—Gordon McDonald

Empty things fill us with frustration. We hate finding the mayonnaise jar empty when we're making a turkey sandwich. We get upset when we're twenty minutes late for an appointment across town and the fuel gauge reads empty. We might even cry if we're in the desert in the middle of August and we reach for our canteen only to find it's empty.

We furnish empty rooms, feed empty stomachs, and fill empty lives with as much pizzazz and activity as we possibly can. Who wants an empty bank account, an empty mailbox, or an empty closet? There's a good reason we don't get enthused about emptiness. We are made in the image of God!

God has a history of filling things and keeping them filled. In less than a week, he filled space with stars, the earth with plants, the sky with clouds, and the sea with fish. He liked that so much that he filled wombs with babies, cities with people, temples with glory, jars with oil, nets with fish, baskets with bread, bodies with life, hearts with gladness, the hungry with food, the weary with rest, the panicked with peace, and the lonely with love. Just about the only empty thing he seemed to approve of was a tomb. But that was because his goal was to fill us up, forever, with himself.

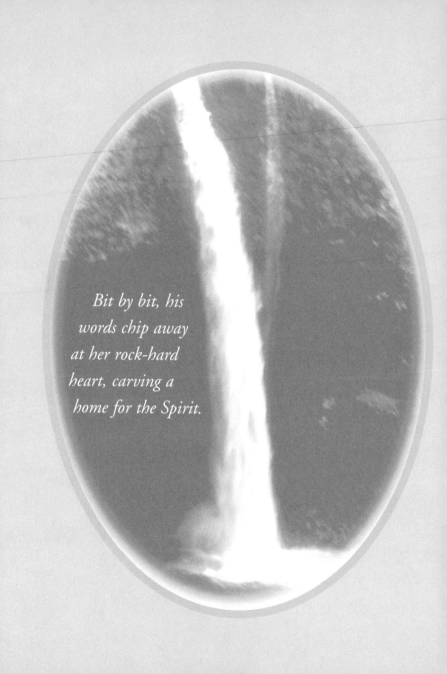

Bit by bit, his words chip away at her rock-hard heart, carving a home for the Spirit.

Where Do You Go to Get Filled?

She plows through her work with her brain in a haze. Hers aren't the kind of duties that require much thinking. The chores never change. She doesn't even need a clock to mark her days. According to the job at hand, it's already noon. So the woman tightens her sandals, grabs a bucket and an empty jar from the corner, and walks out, shutting the door behind her.

Heat rises from the ground, making mountains shimmer in the distance. Sweat trickles down her neck as she stops to knock gravel from her shoes.

Good. No one else is on the road.

The others will come later, when it's cooler—after she's home and out of reach of their insults.

Her man is a laborer. He's more demanding than all her children put together. And he drinks too much. At least once a week she threatens to throw him out. But he pays the bills and sometimes, pays attention to her, so she puts up with him. Because of him and the parade of men before him, she's unwelcome in her neighbors' homes and they talk behind her back.

The well is at the end of the road, and she sees a man sitting there. A stranger? He seems to be resting. Since he has no animals or water bucket, the woman decides he must be traveling. But then she gets close enough to see his face, and she wants to spit. The man is more than a stranger. He's an enemy.

Who does he think he is?

He's obviously a Jew—one who despises the mixed heritage of her people, who insists they have no hope for resurrection and treats them like dogs or, worse, Gentiles.

He must be a fugitive, in a hurry to get to Galilee, or lost. No righteous Jew would ever pass through here unless he had to.

But Jesus knows exactly where he is, and the journey here has made him hot and tired and thirsty. His disciples have gone into town for food while he sits, meditating and waiting like Abraham's servant did at another well long ago. He's waiting for his disciples and for anyone else the Father might send to him.

The woman flings her leather bucket into the well and listens for the sound of a splat at the bottom. When the bucket feels heavy enough, she tightens her grip on the rope and hauls it seventy-five feet back to the top. Then she pours the water into the jar.

The water looks good to Jesus. His throat is dry—

almost as dry, he thinks, as this woman's soul. So he says, "Will you give me a drink?"

The woman nearly drops her jar.

What's this? A Jew speaks to me? Did he ask me for a drink? Jews don't drink with Samaritans.

"Why are you, a Jew, asking me, a Samaritan woman, for a drink?" she answers him.

It's a slap in the face, but Jesus doesn't flinch. He sees this woman, out of sync with society, spurned by her own rejected people. She has more enemies than friends and more weariness than rest. She has never seen the good life and wouldn't even know it if it stared her in the face. Looking at her, Jesus sees how multiplied sadness has hardened her heart, and his melts. He says, "If you knew the gift God has for you, and who I am, you would be asking me for a drink, and I would give you fresh, living water."

She hadn't expected this. A kind-talking Jew. The woman is intrigued. *What does he mean, "living water"?*

24

Changing her tone, she says, "Sir, you don't even have a bucket, and this well is deep. How are you going to get this living water?"

Jesus leaks a faint smile. Then he points to the well and says, "Those who drink this water will get thirsty again. But anyone who drinks the water I give will never thirst. My water is like a spring that never runs dry."

He has her attention now. A kind-talking, spring-promising Jew! She's fascinated and decides to play along. "Sir, give me this water so I won't ever get thirsty or have to come to this well again!"

Jesus looks her straight in the eye and says, "Go call your husband and come back."

Aha! He's a salesman of some kind! He wants me to get my husband so he can close the deal. Well, he won't get a penny out of me.

Then, lifting the water jar to her hip, she answers, "I have no husband."

Jesus squints into the sun, then chuckles and says,

"You're absolutely correct when you say you have no husband. You've had five husbands, and the man you're living with now is not your husband."

Stunned, the woman shifts the weight of her jar, then looks out at the mountains.

How could he know? No one in town even knows the number of husbands I've had. Dear Lord! He's not a salesman. He's a prophet! What do I say now? . . . Something religious.

"Sir, I can see that you're a prophet. So tell me about this issue of where to worship. We worship on that mountain, but the Jews say we should go to Jerusalem."

Jesus knows the woman is like everyone else, worried about form, not fellowship, stuck on rituals, clueless about relationship. "Believe me, woman, a time is coming when . . . " Drop by drop, he lets her taste the radical new drink he's offering the world. Bit by bit, his words chip away at her rock-hard heart, carving a home for the Spirit.

What kind of prophet is this?

He makes her thirsty for God. His words are truth like she's never heard it. But the truth he shares is so deep and it comes so fast that when he's done speaking she says, "I don't know about all you've said. But I do know the Messiah is coming. And when he comes, everything will make sense."

She has faith Jesus can't ignore. If she believes this much in the Messiah and trusts his every word, she should be rewarded with the full revelation. It doesn't matter that she's an immoral woman and a Samaritan or that he hasn't even spoken like this to his disciples.

Jesus looks steadily at her and says, "I am he."

The woman steps back.

Did he say? . . .

Her heart pounds, but before she can speak, the disciples return. They didn't hear what Jesus had said, but they recognize who he's talking to. They keep quiet, but their dropped jaws speak for themselves. The woman looks at Jesus' disciples, then back to him. His face hasn't changed.

He's not joking! He said he's the Messiah!

The woman takes off in such a rush that she leaves her water at the well. All the way home she replays the scene in her head and laughs a nervous, excited laugh under her breath.

Go call your husband . . . He knew the whole time! The man is a Jew but certainly like no Jew I've ever met. And he talked to me like I was someone. He didn't despise me; he received me. We know the Christ is coming. What if he's telling the truth? What does it mean that he spoke to me, confided in me? Me, of all people.

First she finds her man. Then she looks for her children. Finally she shocks her neighbors. Boldness bubbles up from within, and she tells them everything Jesus had said. Before long, a crowd has gathered at the well because Samaritans are curious people, just like everyone else.

Two days later, it's noontime again, and the Savior visits the woman's house while the whole town knocks on her door and an old water jar sits empty in the corner.

*W*here do you go to get filled?

You may not draw from a well, but every day you go somewhere—to that place you hope will fix you or make you feel better or help you forget. Where do you go? Is it the office or the pantry or the mall or the gym? Do you draw your strength from people or lick your lips on a dream? Each time you go for the gusto, remember, Christ will be there too. And when you least expect it, he'll ask: "Does this really satisfy you?"

Do you have an unquenchable thirst? Drop your bucket into Living Water. Drop it down deep, until it sloshes over when you pull it back up. Then . . . dip your hand down in it. Let it satisfy your heart. This water gushes like a geyser. Sip it; savor it. Stick your tongue down into it. Swallow it. Splash in it. Slurp up the spray. Swim in it. Float in it. Bathe your whole life in it. Once you've tasted and tried it, you can't stay away.

Scriptural Account

[Jesus] came to a town in Samaria called Sychar, near the plot of ground Jacob had given to his son Joseph. Jacob's well was there, and Jesus, tired as he was from the journey, sat down by the well. It was about the sixth hour.

When a Samaritan woman came to draw water, Jesus said to her, "Will you give me a drink?" (His disciples had gone into the town to buy food.)

The Samaritan woman said to him, "You are a Jew and I am a Samaritan woman. How can you ask me for a drink?" (For Jews do not associate with Samaritans.)

Jesus answered her, "If you knew the gift of God and who it is that asks you for a drink, you would have asked him and he would have given you living water."

"Sir," the woman said, "you have nothing to draw with and the well is deep. Where can you get this living water? Are you greater than our father Jacob, who gave us the well and drank from it himself, as did also his sons and his flocks and herds?"

Jesus answered, "Everyone who drinks this water will be thirsty again, but whoever drinks the water I give him will never thirst. Indeed, the water I give him will become in him a spring of water welling up to eternal life."

The woman said to him, "Sir, give me this water so that I won't get thirsty and have to keep coming here to draw water."

He told her, "Go, call your husband and come back."

"I have no husband," she replied.

Jesus said to her, "You are right when you say you have no husband. The fact is, you have had five husbands, and the man you now have is not your husband. What you have just said is quite true."

31

"Sir," the woman said, "I can see that you are a prophet. Our fathers worshiped on this mountain, but you Jews claim that the place where we must worship is in Jerusalem."

Jesus declared, "Believe me, woman, a time is coming when you will worship the Father neither on this mountain nor in Jerusalem. You Samaritans worship what you do not know; we worship what we do know, for salvation is from the Jews. Yet a time is coming and has now come when the true worshipers will worship the Father in spirit and truth, for they are the kind of worshipers the Father seeks. God is spirit, and his worshipers must worship in spirit and in truth."

The woman said, "I know that Messiah" (called Christ) "is coming. When he comes, he will explain everything to us."

Then Jesus declared, "I who speak to you am he."

Just then his disciples returned and were surprised to find him talking with a woman. But no one asked,

"What do you want?" or "Why are you talking with her?"

Then, leaving her water jar, the woman went back to the town and said to the people, "Come, see a man who told me everything I ever did. Could this be the Christ?"

—*John 4:5–29*

three

His
Receiving
Embrace

No one is beyond the scope of my touch. I delight in rescuing the needy who cry out. I'm here to deliver those who have no one else to help. For the sake of my great name I won't reject you, because I was so pleased to make you my own.

Your Great Physician
—from Matthew 19:26; Psalm 72:12; 1 Samuel 12:22

Embraced by the Savior

"Jesus is a friend who walks in when the world has walked out."
—author unknown

*M*aybe you've had your credit card declined, your help refused, or your feelings discounted. Perhaps you've seen your opinions shot down, your application thrown out, your entry barred, or your membership denied. You may even have had a friendship renounced, a proposal rebuffed, wisdom spurned, or your love unreturned.

There's a chance you've had your warnings unheeded, your contributions unrecognized, or your work unrewarded. You may have been turned down because you weren't smart enough or sent away because you weren't wanted. But there's one thing you've never been: *you've never been rejected by*

Jesus. In fact, before you were born, God wanted you. And now that you're here, he can't get enough of you.

Have you gotten a pink slip from your employer or been brushed off by a neighbor? Were you scorned by a teacher or compared to a brother? Have you been eliminated from a competition or felt a door slam in your face? Do you know how it feels to be ignored by your mother, jilted by a lover, or forgotten by a friend?

You've endured much and will endure much more, but because of Christ, there's one thing you will never have to feel—God's rejection. Isaiah 41:9–10 says, "I have chosen you and have not rejected you. So do not fear, for I am with you."

Christ is an unconditional includer. And he promises to remain unreasonably, irrationally, and irrevocably devoted to you, no matter what anyone else may say, do, or think.

The man's ragged clothes and foul complexion lodge like arrows in the Lord's heart, wounding and weighing it down with compassion.

I Am Willing

Why should he get up? He has no place to go, no boss to please, no dreams to chase. He rolls over and shuts his eyes. Maybe if he goes back to sleep, he won't have to watch himself die. Then he remembers. His wife is coming.

Twice a week, without fail, she comes out to see him. He should feel lucky. She hasn't abandoned him like the wives of some other men here. But then, she's always been stronger than most women, and more beautiful. He should feel lucky. Instead, he feels rotten.

He'd like to blame someone. The priest? But the priest had only done his job when he'd sent the man into isolation for a two-week waiting period. "Just a precaution," the priest had said. But during the two weeks the man's condition had not improved. His whole world went black. The priest pronounced him "unclean" and sentenced him to life in the caves with the other curse-carriers.

"I'm sorry. I have to do this. It's the law," the priest had said.

Sitting up, the man explores his scalp with his fingers until they find a festering sore. Bigger, he notes. Some days his disease creeps along, unnoticed like a giant glacier. Sometimes it's a man-eater, chewing through his face and hands like a glutton.

"Got any food in here?" asks a toothless beggar, scrounging through the man's food bag.

"Keep your dirty hands off that!" the man yells, grabbing his bag and stuffing it under his blanket.

"What's the matter, boy?" the old man cackles. "Afraid you might catch leprosy? Better watch out for that leprosy. It'll eat your lunch," he howls and hobbles off.

Outside, the man pitches rocks at a bush while he waits for his wife. After every other toss, he glances up at the ridge. Where is she? She usually comes early, carting his food and wine. The man doesn't eat in front of her though. Instead, he drinks in her hair, savors her smile, and tastes her cheeks with his eyes. He hasn't held her in five years. Each time she leaves, he begs her not to return. But she always says, "Don't talk foolishness," and comes back anyway.

A mile away, in the village, a crowd swarms around a young girl sitting on her mother's lap. It's a curious scene. Laughing and crying, the mother rocks the child in her arms. The daughter looks bewildered.

"Only God could do this," whispers one man to another.

"This child has been blind since birth," a woman announces, "but today she can see! Praise God! He's finally sent a prophet!"

Then the crowd rushes off to find the man who gave sight to the blind girl. Everyone needs a miracle. But who knows how many miracles God will allot per day? If they hurry, maybe they can reach him before all his power dries up.

Still waiting near the caves, the man aims another rock and smacks a branch dead on. What's keeping his wife? She's never this late. *Maybe she's not coming,* mocks a voice in his head. *Maybe she's tired of walking so far to see your scabby face. Or maybe,* the voice stabs and twists like a knife, *she's found someone else.* The man flings a rock into the blinding sun. Then he turns to head back down the ravine.

"Wait!" calls a voice behind him. "Honey, don't go!"

Horrified, the man watches his wife sprint down the

steep path, past the safe zone, until she stops, out of breath, dangerously close to him.

"What are you doing? Get back!" the man yells, covering his mouth with his sleeve.

"I know I'm late. I'm sorry. But something remarkable is happening in the village," his wife says, wild-eyed. "I've come to get you. You must see this."

"Are you crazy? You know I can't leave here," the man says.

"Trust me," she pleads. "You have to come with me, right now, before he's gone!"

"What are you talking about? Before who's gone?"

"I've seen a man. Some say he's a prophet, I don't know. But everyone he touches is healed. I'm telling you, I've seen it with my own eyes. Just now, a little blind girl . . . The most amazing thing I've ever seen. So, I thought, if he can heal a blind girl . . . "

"Did you see him heal a leper?"

"Well, no. But why not a leper? I'm telling you, this

man has incredible power. Please, come with me. What do we have left to lose? If for no other reason, do it for me."

By now, villagers have flopped down and sprawled out in front of a merchant's house. Toddlers nurse. Tradesmen bicker. Teenagers nap. Every few minutes, a different voice rises above the murmur shouting, "Jesus! Come out!"

Finally, the door jerks open. Right there, in full view of the clueless people stands the Son of the Living God. People scramble to their feet as disciples spill out of the doorway and form a wedge. They lock arms and clear a path for their teacher through the sea of hands. Then they freeze, startled by the image before them. Out of the shadows walks a highly contagious leper.

The sick man panics in the middle of the street. Quickly, he covers his mouth with his dirty sleeve and shouts the warning, "Unclean! Unclean!" Fear scatters the villagers as if bullets had been shot through the crowd. Even the disciples back off until only Jesus is left standing ten feet from the man.

The Great Physician doesn't ask his patient where it hurts. Leprosy speaks for itself. It makes a meal of a body: It eats away self-worth, chews a man's chances, and devours his destiny. The man's ragged clothes and foul complexion lodge like arrows in the Lord's heart, wounding and weighing it down with compassion.

Jesus surveys the empty street, then folds his hands against his chest. He raises his eyebrows and invites the man closer with a smile.

The man gasps like a fish out of water. His heart flaps and flutters. His thoughts jumble. Why is this total stranger taking such a risk? What if nothing happens? Why had he listened to his wife? But the look in Jesus' eyes quiets all his frantic questions. Dropping his sleeve from his mouth, the man bows his head, sinks to his knees, and says, "If you are willing, you can make me clean."

Looking down on his head, Jesus spots a whitish sore. He takes a deep breath and lifts his right hand—the mighty right hand of God, gloved for the moment in tough, callous skin, the same hand that will be punctured for every plague and stabbed for every sin. He lifts that hand, the hand of the Lamb, and does an unthinkable thing. He lays it flat on the sore, jolting every dead cell in the man's body. Then he nods and says kindly, "I am willing. Be clean!"

Instantly, a flash of warmth washes from the man's head, across his face, and down to his palms. Infections seal shut. White hairs turn black, and his skin yanks tight like a drawstring. Then the same potent power that restored his flesh scours out the contamination in his soul.

"Oh, Lord. Oh, my Lord!" the man moans in amazement, sliding his hands down his arms. "It's gone. All gone." He searches his body. "Look! Every bit of it is gone!"

The man's wife races from the shadows. She circles him, her eyes pooling tears, repeating over and over, "My Lord and my God!"

Then it happens. The man does what he thought he'd never get to do again. Cleansed and free, he reaches for his wife's hand and pulls her into his arms.

Stunned and cautious, the crowd trickles back. Is it true? Leprosy? Cured? By nightfall, the whole town is singing and dancing and celebrating. They seat the man at the head table, and everyone competes for a chance to sit next to him.

*C*hrist gave the ultimate reception to a man who expected rejection. When the rest of the world ran from him, the King of kings drew closer in. When the situation seemed terminal, God produced a miracle.

Do you have a wound that won't heal? There is hope. You may live in a different time, lead a different life, or long for a different cure than the leper, but you share the same Savior. Jesus is the same, yesterday, today, and forever. There's no sickness he hasn't seen or sin he can't forgive. Tell him the whole story. Let him know where you hurt. Then ask the Great Physician to touch those tender, hidden places of your heart and renew your prescription for joy. Let him clean out your bitterness, purify your perspective, and launder your life with his love. Step out from the shadows today. He's waiting. Know that he'll never refuse you. He's willing to make you clean.

Scriptural Account

A man with leprosy came to him and begged him on his knees, "If you are willing, you can make me clean."

Filled with compassion, Jesus reached out his hand and touched the man. "I am willing," he said. "Be clean!" Immediately the leprosy left him and he was cured.

—Mark 1:40–42

four

His
Renewing
Embrace

I see you struggling, and I know the anguish of your soul. I know it seems as if I've forgotten you, but your troubles are only temporary. After you have suffered for a while, I'll personally restore you and make you strong, firm, and steadfast. You'll be amazed by the brilliance of my eternal glory that will be revealed in you.

Your God of All Grace

—from Psalm 22:24; 31:7; 2 Corinthians 4:17; 1 Peter 5:10

Embraced by the Savior

"Diseases can be our spiritual flat tires—disruptions in our lives that seem to be disasters at the time but end by redirecting our lives in a meaningful way."

—Bernie S. Siegel

If you browse *Reader's Digest* or go to the movies or watch much TV, you're bound to notice our fascination with rescue stories. It doesn't matter if it's actual late-breaking news or a celluloid fantasy: Emergencies, catastrophes, last-second escapes, and life-threatening recoveries captivate us. They make us hold our breath, grip the armrest, drop our newspaper, and phone the neighbors. We're rescue hungry, and the thought of someone trapped in a mine or lost at sea or stuck out in space excites our senses.

Fortunately, Christ is absorbed with rescues too. You might say they're his passion. He's so committed to them that he's put a sign on his wall in big red letters that reads: "Let No One Perish!" His rescues cover every kind of crisis and span several thousand years. So, if you find yourself flailing, trust him. He's even been known to do miracles.

Are you hanging by a thread? Summon the Savior. Tied to the track and a train's coming fast? Recruit the Redeemer. You won't have to beg or twist his arm. He was made for this. In fact, when the Father told him about the mess you're in, Christ said he was dying to save you.

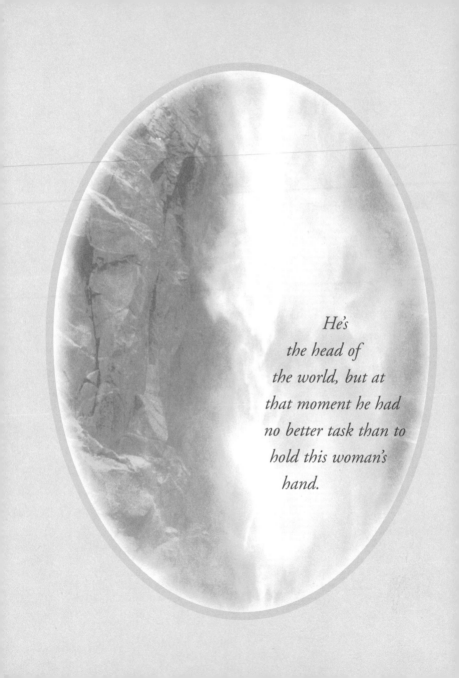

*He's
the head of
the world, but at
that moment he had
no better task than to
hold this woman's
hand.*

He'll Come to You

The first thing you notice is not the dark brown eyes or slate-gray hair or the sagging layers of skin below her chin. She has a kind face and a matter-of-fact mouth, but neither of them really grabs your attention. What catches your eye is her hands.

They are hands on a hunt—nonstop, never-rest hands. They're smooth and bony, and they flutter and fly around the house like a pair of hungry hawks. Combing and clasping, stirring and sweeping, washing and wiping, every day the woman's hands carry out a sovereign strategy. From dawn to dusk, they triumphantly box at the shadow that falls late in the day of a woman's life. Whatever these hands find to do, they do it with all their might.

Why does she do it? Has she always been this motivated? No. For years she thought the best days of her life had sifted away like sand through an hourglass.

The woman sleeps in a converted storage room at the back of her son-in-law's house. It's a far cry from what she'd been used to, but she keeps her complaints to a minimum. After her husband's death, debts forced her to sell the home they'd shared for more than twenty years. Her only remaining possessions were her clothes and a few pieces of family furniture. At least she still had their bed—and their daughter, who took her in.

Soon after moving in with her daughter, the two of them were working together in the kitchen when the woman began to feel cold. Every few minutes a creeping shiver worked its way up her back and out the top of her head. Finally, she looked around and asked, "Did someone leave the door open?"

"No. The door's closed," her daughter answered.

"Well, it's cold in here," the woman said, annoyed.

"Cold? Mother, we've been baking for hours. Are you feeling all right?"

"I'm telling you, this house is either too hot or too cold. If that husband of yours stayed home more often, maybe he'd have time to do something about it," the woman complained, dusting flour off her hands. "I'll be back."

Taking a deep breath, the daughter shook her head and removed a hot loaf of bread from the oven. Her mother could be difficult to live with, but the girl understood how hard it must be to accept her help. And, with her husband's travel, the daughter appreciated her mother's company.

In her room, the woman lifted the lid on a wooden box in search of a warm woolen tunic. As she stooped to sort through the clothes, she felt a tightness in her forehead. She reached for a chair as the room started to swirl. She tried to focus. The room still turned. She stood up straight. That made her feel worse.

Inching her way across the floor, the woman reached for the edge of the bed. If she could just lie down . . . but the spinning continued, and she had no power to stop it.

In the kitchen her daughter called out, "Mother! You aren't leaving the cleanup for me, are you?"

But the woman didn't hear. Her eyes burned in their sockets, her head throbbed, and her muscles ached. She couldn't remember ever feeling this ill. She didn't dare move. Shivers turned to shakes. Her temperature climbed.

"Mother?" her daughter asked from the foot of the bed, "are you sick?"

"Get me a blanket," she answered through chattering teeth.

Touching her mother's cheek the daughter became alarmed by the heat. "You're burning up," she said. "I'll get a cold cloth."

Every hour the woman's fever stoked hotter. And all night the daughter sat by her mother's side, wiping her face with cool cloths and calming her with prayers. The woman ached too much to sleep, and she was much too sick to talk. At times she moaned, delirious.

By sunrise the daughter was spent, and the woman hadn't improved. When would the fever break? The daughter needed sleep, but it was the Sabbath. Her husband would want a meal when he and his brother returned from the synagogue. And he would probably bring a guest.

Later, through her sickness, the woman heard booming voices from what seemed like another world. She couldn't distinguish them. They were muffled and noisy and getting closer. Abruptly they halted. In her fog, she sensed people in the room.

"Mother," the daughter said softly, "Simon has brought someone to see you."

Jesus stood in the doorway. He'd been summoned to the scene like a lifeguard at the beach. "Hurry, there's a lady down there, and she's sinking fast!" the bystanders yelled. That's why he was here. He's a Savior. And he'd come to yank another victim from the deep.

A minor multitude trailed behind him into the room. James and John, the daughter, her husband, Simon, and his brother Andrew all squeezed into the old converted storage room.

Simon leaned against a wall with a nervous grin. Sure he had witnessed the wine at the wedding. But that had been a special occasion. And yes, he'd watched that very morning as Jesus freed a man from demons at the synagogue. If a miracle was going to happen anywhere, you'd expect it in the house of God. But this was his house, and the sick woman was his mother-in-law—neither one particularly special or holy.

Jesus stepped to the side of the bed and lifted the woman's wrinkled hand into the hollow of his own. Looking past her face, through her skin, he saw her in a way no one else could. He saw her idleness, her loneliness, and the untapped potential of the years she had left. He's the head of the world, but at that moment he had no better task than to hold this woman's hand.

Then he dismissed the fever with a firm rebuke.

It was quick and painless. Five, ten, twenty seconds passed as layer by layer the woman was pulled up until she broke through the surface of the fever. Silver sweat dripped from her neck, leaving spots on her clothes. Her eyes opened.

"Mother!" her daughter cried.

"Master!" the disciples shouted when the woman sat up, relaxed and refreshed, as if she'd only been napping.

The woman stared. She blinked. What had happened here? Just a moment ago . . . But now her cheeks were cool; her head was clear. She felt strong, no, better than strong. She looked up. What was this? Heaven had hold of her hand.

She had fallen into bed with a fever and awakened with a future. What had started as a sickness carved a trail to the Savior. And from just one touch, the Lord of Life had created a grateful servant from a weary old woman.

"Why is everyone just standing around?" she finally asked after Jesus helped her up. "What time is it anyway? You boys look hungry. Come with me. I'll fix you a meal that you'll never forget."

When you're too sick to seek help, remember this: Christ still makes house calls. Even to tiny back rooms. Even to your room. Chances are good that he's already there, waiting for you. Even if all you can do is lie there, he'll come to you. He'll step into your world, stand by your side, and hold tight to your hand—for as long as it takes to heal your aches or ease your mind and get you back on track.

Then, share your relief and serve someone else. Because when God touches a hand, he gives it a task. That's when ordinary chores become acts of worship. How will he want you to praise him?

Scriptural Account

Jesus left the synagogue and went to the home of Simon. Now Simon's mother-in-law was suffering from a high fever, and they asked Jesus to help her. So he bent over her and rebuked the fever, and it left her. She got up at once and began to wait on them.

—Luke 4:38–39

five

His Redeeming Embrace

At one time you were alienated from me, separated because of your sin. But Jesus made peace between us by shedding his blood on the cross. Because of his death, you've been reconciled to me. You're holy in my sight, without blemish. No one can accuse you. There's no condemnation. You've been pardoned.

Your Judge & Heavenly Father

—from Colossians 1:20–22

Embraced by the Savior

"Decisions can take you out of God's will but never out of his reach."
—author unknown

We've all done things we're not particularly proud of, things we'd never want people to know about. These are actions we'd never want flashed on *CNN Headline News* or tossed around at the water cooler. They create a sinking, sickening feeling when we drive down a particular street or see a certain date on the calendar.

Maybe we stole something or cheated an employer. Perhaps we were foolish or careless or heartless or selfish. Maybe we lied or were unfaithful.

We've all done a thing or two we wish we could forget.

But sometimes, even when we know we've been forgiven, forgetting isn't all that easy. There's an accuser out there, making it his business to flaunt our failures. This accuser never forgets a face or a fact or a fault. And as long as he has enough power to pester, he'll continue to bring up these past deeds we're not particularly proud of.

Thankfully, God gives us the remedy for the devil's ridicule—a way to shut his blabbering mouth and live at peace within ourselves. The remedy is this: *Remember no sin that God himself has chosen to forget.* Satan records our wrongs, but the Savior erases the tape. Don't give the enemy room to reign in your brain. Practice the Savior's art of selective amnesia for forgiven sins. And if you need help, try this: Tie a string around your pointing finger so you'll remember to forget.

His
words pound
the woman's heart.
They crack it open,
feeding it warmth and
light, bringing it back
from death.

No Stones to Throw

In the hours before dawn, a woman sits in her cell, barefoot and half-dressed. She runs her finger up and down a jagged crack in the cold stone floor. Over and over she traces the crevice until her finger is raw and numb. Tears streak her face. She's exhausted, but fear of what the sunrise will bring has stolen her sleep.

It's been a long night. No. Make that a long life. This night is just one last bitter bite from the whole rotten apple. How could she have been so stupid? Why hadn't she been more careful? All night she's tried to figure out how they knew where to find her.

However it came about, she was found—they were found—asleep together. The woman had kicked and scratched and bitten the guards. They had yanked her hair and slapped her face. She remembered spitting at one while another jabbed her with the point of his spear. That's when she'd noticed he was gone. Maybe her lover had gotten away. More likely they'd let him escape. The dogs! They lock her up and let him go. What kind of justice is that?

"What kind of justice?" an official had shouted when she protested. "I'll tell you what kind. We have witnesses who say you tempted him! You're responsible for this wickedness, and in a few hours we'll see that you pay for it."

Not far away, in the temple courts, the eager ones trickle in before daybreak. Never mind the hour. Never mind that the feast is over and their families and businesses are waiting. Rumor has it the teacher will be back again today, creating more controversy, making more outrageous claims and infuriating the learned leaders of the law.

"What do you think he'll say today?" one man asks.

"I don't know. I've heard some say he's the Christ. But how can the Christ come from Galilee?" another replies.

Pacing back and forth, the woman pulls a bed scarf around her shoulders. But it's too thin to keep her warm. She had always thought she'd die of old age. She'd seen a man stoned once. Well, actually, she had heard his screams for mercy and the horrible thump of stones gouging skin. She had wanted to see, but her mother had covered her eyes. Thinking of her mother brings more tears.

But thinking of her stepfather brings only wrath. If he had let her marry the one she loved, she wouldn't be here. But he had denied her. To him, she was like one of his animals. Only his animals got better treatment. When time had come for marriage, he traded her like a piece of property to another heartless man twice her age.

At dawn, the teacher and his disciples come down from the olive groves outside the city. As he walks, a woman hands him some bread for his breakfast. He smiles and nods, then breaks the loaf and eats half, dropping the other half in the empty hand of a beggar at the temple gate.

"He's coming! I see him!" someone shouts.

A moment later Jesus enters the temple as welcome and regal as a prince. People flock to him, arms fluttering, like moths drawn to a flame. They think it's because he's a celebrity. But Jesus knows different. This is how it has always been and will always be in the presence of God.

When Jesus sits down, his eyes wander over the crowd. It's a mixed lot. Disciples and doubters, followers and faultfinders, supporters and skeptics. If he wanted, he could make quite a show of exposing the secrets of their souls. But he has more important thoughts to reveal and more amazing secrets to tell.

Jesus opens his mouth to speak, and the buzz of the crowd lowers to a hush.

In a dark corridor, a guard shoves the woman and says, "Let's go!"

"Where are you taking me?" she asks in terror.

"Shut up and walk," he says.

A small horde of religious lawyers and priests wait outside for the woman. They've conspired and consulted and think, perhaps, they can kill two birds with one stone today. Or, better yet, one bird and a big fish. The woman is bait for the fish. When she finally appears, they sneer with disgust, then march ahead of her.

In the temple, Jesus is well into his teaching when the scribes and Pharisees storm the courtyard.

"Now what?" a disciple wonders under his breath.

Jesus knows these men, some for a long time. He's eaten in some of their homes, talked privately with others.

When he was just twelve years old, he sat with several in these very halls discussing the law and the prophets. The rulers appear rattled and barge up to the teacher like they own the place. Curious, he gets up to meet them.

Then Jesus sees the woman pulled along behind them, panic-stricken and humiliated. One of the Pharisees motions to a guard. He thrusts the woman before the crowd. Clutching her scarf, she hangs her head in shame.

Murmurs rustle around her. Some in the crowd crane their necks or stand on their toes to get a better view.

"Teacher," a scribe begins, "this woman was caught in the act of adultery. In the Law, Moses commanded us to stone such women. Now what do you say?"

The woman stares at her feet, shaking and confused. What's this about? Why do they consult this man? Why should they care what he thinks?

Slowly Jesus squats down and begins to draw on the ground with his finger.

"What's he drawing?" a merchant whispers.

"I can't see," another answers.

"Jesus, did you hear the question?" the scribe repeats, agitated. "What do you think we should do with her?"

Jesus doesn't flinch. His finger loops and swirls in a thin layer of sand. It's a curious sight. It draws all eyes to him instead of the woman.

"Stop playing games with us, Jesus. If you don't have an answer, then be man enough to say so," another scribe says.

After a long pause, Jesus straightens up, folding his arms across his chest. With a laser-sharp glare, he studies each Pharisee. Then, he says firmly, "If any one of you is without sin, let him be the first to throw a stone at her." Again, Jesus bends down to write. But what's he writing now? Maybe he's listing names or doodling in the dirt to antagonize them, some think. He could be remembering the words of Job: "For you write down bitter things against me and make me inherit the sins of my youth." Or maybe, just maybe, he's scratching out the first draft of a brand-new covenant.

For a full minute the courtyard is still. Some of the Pharisees look ill. A man in the back clears his throat.

Finally, there's movement from the oldest member of the group. He stares at Jesus for a moment, then walks off, paving the way for possibly the most memorable exodus since Moses walked the Hebrews out of Egypt. One by one, oldest to youngest, the Pharisees disperse, defeated, empty-handed, catching neither bird nor fish.

When they've gone, Jesus stands up, turns to the woman, and says, "Woman, where are they? Has no one condemned you?"

The woman blinks in disbelief and answers, "No one, sir."

But there is one left who could demand her death. She doesn't understand that it is the sinless Son of God who speaks to her. But instead of striking her down or ridiculing her before the crowd, he comes as the Lord of Love, reaching out to lift the latch on her cage. He says, "Then neither do I condemn you. Go now and leave your life of sin."

The words pound the woman's heart. They crack it open, feeding it warmth and light, bringing it back from death. Not condemned? Does this mean she can go? Does this mean she can live?

The woman looks into the eyes of this stranger, this Savior, for assurance. Then she sees it: all the proof of a pardon she needs. It's there, in the face shining back at her. She feels awkward, unaccustomed to such kindness, such mercy. But it grabs her, gets hold of her. Then it lets her go—free.

Jesus could have condemned the woman, but he chose to redeem her. She had failed greatly, but he granted her favor. He didn't excuse the sin, but he did embrace the sinner.

Is the "accuser of the brethren" trying to convict you? He hasn't got a case. Jesus has already spoken in your defense. Are there sins you just can't forget? The Savior doesn't choose to condemn you, so why do you choose to remember? Yes, the Father knows every unfaithful act, unthinkable deed, and unwholesome thought. He despises sin. But he's devoted to you. Look at his hands. You'll find no stones to throw or ax to grind, only grace to give. No, you don't deserve it, but a gift can never be earned. And no, you can't undo what's done, but you can do this: From here on out, copy Jesus. Cast no stones. Condemn no sinners. And clear your path of those who do. Then go and sin no more.

Scriptural Account

But Jesus went to the Mount of Olives. At dawn he appeared again in the temple courts, where all the people gathered around him, and he sat down to teach them. The teachers of the law and the Pharisees brought in a woman caught in adultery. They made her stand before the group and said to Jesus, "Teacher, this woman was caught in the act of adultery. In the Law Moses commanded us to stone such women. Now what do you say?" They were using this question as a trap, in order to have a basis for accusing him. But Jesus bent down and started to write on the ground with his finger. When they kept on questioning him, he straightened up and said to them, "If any one of you is without sin, let him be the first to throw a stone at her." Again he stooped down and wrote on the ground.

At this, those who heard began to go away one at a time, the older ones first, until only Jesus was left, with the woman still standing there. Jesus straightened up and asked her, "Woman, where are they? Has no one condemned you?"

"No one, sir," she said.

"Then neither do I condemn you," Jesus declared. "Go now and leave your life of sin."

—*John 8:1–11*

six

His Reviving Embrace

Know that I hear you and am merciful to you. Watch me transform mourning into dancing. I take your rags of despair and dress you radiantly with my inexpressible joy.

Your God of All Comfort

—*from Psalm 30:10–12; 1 Peter 1:2–3*

Embraced by the Savior

"We are uncertain of the next step but we are certain of God. You can be certain that he will come."

—Oswald Chambers

Remember what it was like to learn how to drive, how you crept along under the speed limit gripping the wheel with both hands? Remember concentrating so hard to stay between the curb and the centerline that you couldn't see past the front bumper? And if someone pointed at something down the road, you didn't dare look because you thought you'd crash.

Learning to "drive in the Spirit" has the same intensity. Fear and inexperienced faith often cause us to frantically grip the wheel of our lives; sometimes we just stall in the middle of the road. But every time we focus on where we are or how bad things look, we're blind to the horizon where God is at work.

King David had his share of challenges, yet he overcame them because he knew where to look for help: "I lift up my eyes to the hills—where does my help come from? My help comes from the Lord." The prophet Elijah told his servant to "look toward the sea" as he waited for confirmation that God would send rain. And Joshua told the people of Israel they must look past the Jordan to view the Promised Land.

Has your "driving" been tested lately? Were you relaxed and steady or tense and reckless? Take a tip from those who have been there: Keep your eyes on the road and your faith toward the future. It will smooth a rough ride through the present.

She would give anything to have back all the nights she'd spent rocking and jostling and coaxing those sweet eyes to sleep.

Keep Your Eyes
on the Road

From a distance they look like two mobs of gunslingers striding toward a showdown on a hot, dusty road. One group wears black, the other white. But as the crowds approach each other, it's clear neither is expecting a shootout between good and evil.

The mob in black is large, loud, and disheveled looking. Some have rips in their clothes and dirt on their distraught and disoriented faces. The women's hair hangs wild and whichever way. They clink and smack instruments between ear-splitting shrieks, like hunters scaring animals out of the bush.

The crowd in white moves toward them. Scattered loosely, they take up the whole road, fanning out across the landscape a half-mile wide. Children play chase, mothers bundle babies, old men step along slowly with walking sticks. Some sing; some chatter in excited tones. If there's any significance to this day, none of them seem to realize it.

The men in black haul a stretcher on poles over their shoulders bearing an open coffin. They're stonefaced and mute and seem to have given the grieving over to the women, who wail in double portion around them.

There's a body in the coffin, a young man in his late teens. He's wound in sheets and a large handkerchief hides his face.

His mother put the handkerchief there herself, after

she gently traced her fingers over his eyes to close them for the last time. She would give anything to have back all the nights she'd spent rocking and jostling and coaxing those sweet eyes to sleep—the eyes she delighted in when he smiled, plucked sand from when he played, rinsed soap from when he washed, and wiped tears from when he hurt. Those bright, dazzling eyes were now shut forever.

When he was younger, his mother walked in front to guide and protect him. Today, she staggers and stumbles behind him crying, "Oh, my son. Oh, my son. My beautiful, beautiful boy." He rides on ahead, oblivious to her moans and to the sky above him and the jerking boards beneath him. He rides on ahead to the plot she thought would be hers, next to the grave where she buried her husband.

Closer now, the happy, sprawling horde spies the procession. No one needs an explanation. They have seen this many times before. A hush ripples though the crowd in white as an offering for the dead. The quiet alerts the

93

throng's leader, who has been in deep conversation. It's Jesus. He looks up, sensing the oncoming sadness, hearing the clanking tambourines and the sobbing woman. His eyes go soft. Concern washes over his face. For as long as he lives, he'll never get used to the sights and sounds of death. It doesn't exist where he came from.

"Step aside people, let them pass," a man says. And every one moves, except Jesus.

"What's he doing?" a follower asks.

"Be quiet and watch," someone answers.

Walking behind the coffin, Jesus spots the dead boy's mother. The sight of her pain deeply moves him. Maybe he pictures his own mother, less than ten miles from here, and tastes the bitter cup she's destined to drink. Maybe he hears from the Father, "Show this weeping woman I know how it feels to lose your only son." Or maybe he imagines the woman, aimless and numb, shut up, alone in her home. Whatever his reason, whatever he sees, it crushes his heart into action.

94

"Don't cry," he says to her, like a gentle father.

"Does she know this man?" a suspicious friend whispers.

"I don't think so," another replies.

Then Jesus walks to the side of the coffin and touches it, bare-handed. Everyone gasps. By touching the coffin he has broken a strict Jewish law.

The coffin bearers freeze.

"What does he think he's doing?" hisses a woman, incensed.

Then Jesus unleashes a force so strong that the dealer of death can't hang on. Stripping Satan of his most powerful weapon, Jesus turns it back on him. Then with the whole host of heaven cheering him on, he commands, "Young man, I say to you, get up!"

Eyebrows rise. The crowd murmurs. The audacity! But there's a twitch inside the young man's wrappings. And the next moment, the widow's son bolts up in his coffin above the men carrying him, looking like a mummy on a throne.

"Lord!" a disciple cries.

Women and children scream and scatter. Some hide their faces.

The boy is saying something, but they can't hear what because his face remains covered. In terror, the coffin bearers scurry to lower their poles.

"Son? Oh, my Lord! Son!" the mother says with her hand to her mouth.

"How? How?" she stammers. "Oh, my boy! My precious, precious boy!" she repeats, running to snatch away the facecloth. There they are—wide open—those bright, beautiful eyes, awake and aware, smiling right back at her.

"God is with us! God has heard us! I can't believe this. I just can't believe I've seen this," says an old man on his knees.

Pandemonium spreads through the crowd. Some shout. Some are speechless. Some run to town to bring back relatives. The disciples grin and laugh and hug. A few have tears in their eyes.

Jesus, too, is delighted. He loosens the young man's wrappings and helps him out of the box. Then, in sheer joy, he fills the mother's arms with her son.

When the grieving mother set out on the road that day, all she saw was a death box. It filled her view and blurred her vision. She couldn't see it at the time, but an unbelievable miracle was just around the corner.

*H*ave you been on the road to a burial? Is your heart dressed in black, stopped in its tracks? Maybe you can't see him yet. Maybe you're doubled over and can't look up. But Comfort is coming. He's just down the road. The Lord knows where your heart has traveled and the conditions of the highway ahead. Let him take your pain into his almighty hands. He's strong enough to resurrect the dead, yet tender enough to soothe your fragile heart. Watch for him. You can't miss him. He'll be coming for you dressed in white.

Scriptural Account

Soon afterward, Jesus went to a town called Nain, and his disciples and a large crowd went along with him. As he approached the town gate, a dead person was being carried out—the only son of his mother, and she was a widow. And a large crowd from the town was with her. When the Lord saw her, his heart went out to her and he said, "Don't cry."

Then he went up and touched the coffin, and those carrying it stood still. He said, "Young man, I say to you, get up!" The dead man sat up and began to talk, and Jesus gave him back to his mother.

They were all filled with awe and praised God. "A great prophet has appeared among us," they said. "God has come to help his people." This news about Jesus spread throughout Judea and the surrounding country.

—Luke 7:11–17

seven

His Replenishing Embrace

*K*now that I'm working behind the scenes to orchestrate your well-being. Realize that everything good and perfect in your life is from me. The hidden tag reads, "Made in heaven especially for you with love by your Father of Light." And I never change. I've always been and always will be in the blessing business.

Your Generous Father

—from James 1:17; 2 Corinthians 5:20

Embraced by the Savior

"Let God love you through others and let God love others through you."

—D. M. Street

No matter where we live or what job we do or how much money we make, we all share a similar ritual almost every day of every week. At some time or other, we check the mailbox.

Checking the mailbox is always a treat. Ninety-nine out of one-hundred days there will be something waiting in it for us. Sure, we find mostly ads and flyers and bills, but some days we reach into our boxes and find a piece of "good mail" mixed in, like a letter from a special friend, or a just-thinking-of-you note from someone we haven't heard from in a long time. Getting good mail feels like hitting the jackpot or receiving a mini-surprise party. It makes us stand in the street or sit on the porch and smile. Maybe we'll rip the envelope open right there, or maybe we'll tuck it into a pocket, pour a cup of tea, and relish reading it in private.

God sends us good mail every day. Sometimes it's addressed directly to us, but often he sends his best mail to us "in care of" someone else. Maybe he sends it through a spouse or a child. He might use a cherished friend or a total stranger. It's not like he's lost our address. It's more like he's chosen to bring someone else into the loop of his love.

"Be
at peace, precious
child; I will let noth-
ing harm you. Lean on
me, precious child; I
will hold and comfort
you."

Count It as Coming from Heaven

When her son is threatened or in danger, when he's in need or disaster approaches, when he's in over his head or about to hit bottom, a mother will be there for him.

She will be there because of the bond, the mysterious glue that holds the child fast in her heart. The child could be three or thirty-three; it doesn't matter. It's all in the cord—a powerful, threefold cord woven in heaven between the mother, her child, and God.

Mary knows about the cord. For thirty-three years she has experienced its tugs and twists and tests. She can tell of its unspeakable joys, unending delights, and unimaginable depths. Mary knows that the natural thing is for the cord to loosen as the child grows until there is so much slack that neither mother nor child feels a pinch or a snap in the comings and goings of their lives. But this is not her experience with her son. Today the cord jerks her to a place every mother hopes she'll never have to go.

Going there will be the hardest thing she's ever done. But no one could keep her away. Just as it had begun, so it will end—with the three of them: the mother, her son, and his Father. It's labor in reverse, pain at both ends of life. Today she joins the ranks of mothers who have lain down to birth babies and then, much sooner than they had expected, stood up to bury them.

"Are you sure you should go?" Mary's sister asks. "Let us take care of things. Stay here and rest," she continues, soliciting agreement from the others.

But Mary ignores them as she moves slowly around the room getting dressed. Her heart weighs her down like a boulder in her chest. They don't understand. But then, how could they? He's her son. Even though he's come to mean so much more to so many people, he will always be her son.

"Mary, John's outside. He wants to go with us," another Mary says. "We'll all go together, all right?"

Mary nods. She's grateful that at least one of the men will be with them in case there's trouble. She should have known it would be John. He has always known what's needed; he has a supernatural sensitivity to people, especially to her son. She's relieved when he takes her arm and leads her through the crowded streets. She leans on him, borrows from his courage.

John seems solemn but not afraid. He adjusts his grip on Mary as they navigate around people, animals, and other obstacles in the street. He is careful, attentive, and focused on her every comfort. After a while she hears him humming under his breath.

"What's that you're humming?" she asks him.

"It's a little song my mother used to sing. I haven't thought of it in a long time."

"Tell me how it goes."

"Well, the part I remember says, 'Be at peace, precious child; I will let nothing harm you. Lean on me, precious child; I will hold and comfort you.' She used to sing it to me at night when I was afraid."

"It's a sweet song."

John nods, then says, "It always seemed to work. She'd sing the song to me, and the next thing I'd know it would be morning."

The closer the group gets to Golgotha, the weaker Mary feels. Over and over she tries to prepare her heart for what she'll see. She tells herself to trust God. She takes deep breaths to slow the adrenaline rushing through her veins.

"Are you all right?" her sister asks.

"I'm all right," she says.

Then they round a corner and look up.

"Oh, no. Oh, no. Please tell me, no, Lord," Mary groans.

They see Jesus, limp and naked, hanging from spikes nailed to rough-sawn wood. Blood streaks his face, drips from his hands, oozes from his feet. Mary's tears flow uncontrollably. Suddenly the cord between them is stretched beyond the limit of her endurance. She feels a sharp, jabbing pain in her throat. She can barely speak. "Oh, no. Please, God. Please, don't," she chokes. "Don't let them . . . please, God, don't let them do this."

Mary had taken such meticulous care of him, always afraid he might fall on a stick or die from disease. For the world's sake she'd cared for the Savior. She'd sheltered

109

him—too much, Joseph had said. She'd tried to relax and let Jesus do the things boys do, but it had made her nervous. She didn't know if God expected her to protect him, if he had given angels charge concerning him, or if he expected it to be a joint venture. *Where are you now, Father? Why have you hidden your angels?*

Finally, Jesus sees Mary. No longer Mary, his mother, but Mary, the woman. He sees the body that bore him, the lips that kissed him, hands that dressed him, and eyes that more and more over the years had looked across the horizon of Nazareth longing for his return.

One last time, Jesus looks at the woman who has believed in him and encouraged him. She blessed him toward a calling far beyond her own human comprehension. He sees her distress. He hears her despair. But his hands are tied. Or are they?

In agony, Jesus calls to Mary from the cross.

"Dear woman," he says, looking past her to John, "here is your son."

Mary is bleary-eyed, confused. Then she sees him motion to John with his head and say with labored breath, "Here is your mother."

Suddenly Mary knows. The cord between them hasn't been ripped apart; Jesus has cut it himself. He is finished here. And he's saying her time with him is finished too. But what is this he's done? A kindness she can hardly fathom. He's not left his end of the cord dangling but has intentionally passed it on to the disciple he loved.

Sobbing, John moves to Mary's side and wraps his arms around her. He wants Jesus to see his absolute obedience, that, yes, his mother will be in good hands. No greater honor could the master have given him. Tonight he will take Mary home with him, and for the rest of his life he will cherish her like his own mother.

Later, at sundown, as the grieving women leave the place where they had laid the Lord's body, one of them stops, saying, "Listen." Turning toward the sound, they see John walking arm in arm with Mary. He looks up at them, smiles faintly, then continues on just loud enough for them to hear: "Be at peace, precious child, I will let nothing harm you. Lean on me, precious child, I will hold and comfort you."

And the next thing they knew, it was morning.

There are times when each of us needs the comfort of Christ. We regret we weren't there to see him in the flesh or feel his touch or hear his voice. But Jesus proved by his example on the cross that heaven hears our hearts' cries to be held. He knew he couldn't be there for his mother, so he commissioned John to take his place. And he knew he'd no longer be present to heal the hurts of the world, so he set in motion his church, his living body, to be him here until he comes back again.

Need a hug from heaven? Jesus knows you do. And he's provided for your very real need through the people he's placed on the path of your life. He wants you to see his face in their expressions, hear his voice through their words, and know his heart from the kindness they show. Why? Because that's the way God has always communicated his heart. He put his love in Mary. He shared his love through Christ. Now, he sets his love in you for distribution whenever and wherever he needs it in this world. God still uses real people. Let him borrow your smile, your laugh, your arms today. And the next time you're hugged by a human . . . count it as coming from heaven.

Scriptural Account

Near the cross of Jesus stood his mother, his mother's sister, Mary the wife of Clopas, and Mary Magdalene. When Jesus saw his mother there, and the disciple whom he loved standing nearby, he said to his mother, "Dear woman, here is your son," and to the disciple, "Here is your mother." From that time on, this disciple took her into his home.

—John 19:25–27

Moments I have felt the Savior's embrace . . .

Surely I took up your infirmities and carried your sorrows.

—from Isaiah 53:4

_____

_____

_____

_____

_____

_____

_____

_____

_____

_____

_____

_____

_____

_____

_____

_____

_____

_____

Come to me. Drink freely of my life-changing water.

—from Isaiah 55:2

Moments I have felt the Savior's embrace . . .

_____

_____

_____

_____

_____

_____

_____

_____

_____

_____

_____

_____

_____

_____

_____

_____

_____

_____

_____

_____

I'll never stop loving you. Be assured, I won't ever abandon you.

—from Psalm 138:8

_____

_____

_____

_____

_____

_____

_____

_____

_____

_____

_____

_____

_____

_____

_____

_____

_____

_____

_____

I'll restore you and make you strong, firm, and steadfast. You'll be amazed.

–from 1 Peter 5:10

Moments I have felt the Savior's embrace . . .

_____

_____

_____

_____

_____

_____

_____

_____

_____

_____

_____

_____

_____

_____

_____

_____

_____

_____

_____

I, even I, am he who comforts you.

–from Isaiah 51:12

_____

_____

_____

_____

_____

_____

_____

_____

_____

_____

_____

_____

_____

_____

_____

_____

_____

_____

See my hand in everything good and perfect that comes into your life.

—from James 1:17

*M*oments I have felt the Savior's embrace . . .

_____

_____

_____

_____

_____

_____

_____

_____

_____

_____

_____

_____

_____

_____

_____

_____

_____

I didn't send Jesus into the world to condemn you, but to save you and everyone else who believes through him.

—from John 3:17